next level **SOUL**™ *PRESENTS*

WHISPERS
OF THE
SOUL®

A COLLECTION OF SPIRITUAL POEMS
FOR MEDITATION

BY CONNIE H. DEUTSCH

LFH
BOOKS

Next Level Soul™ Presents: Whispers of the Soul® A Collection of Spiritual Poems for Meditation

Cover Art & Book Design: IFH Books
Photography by: Aperture Vintage

Next Level Soul™ is a trademark of IFH Industries, Inc.
All Rights Reserved.

IFH Books - A Division of IFH Industries Inc.
13492 N. Highway 183 #120-757
Austin, TX 78750
www.nextlevelsoul.com/books

Ordering Information:
Quantity sales: Special discounts are available on quantity purchases by corporations, associations and others. For details contact the publisher at the address above.

Orders by US trade bookstores and wholesalers:
Please contact the publisher at the address above.

Printed in the United States of America

ISBN Paperback: 9798985894004
First Edition

DEDICATION

This book is dedicated to the most wonderful family anyone could ever wish for. You have been there for me during the best of times and the worst of times. Your continued love and support have been the foundation of my life. For each member of my family . . .

This book is dedicated in loving memory to my parents, Sylvia and Alvin, who taught me to think for myself, question everything, and not care about public opinion . . . and who then wondered why I was such a difficult child to raise.

Of all the things I have accomplished in this life, the most noteworthy and most gratifying of all, has been giving birth to my son, Bruce, and having him in my life. He is everything a mother could want and I'm proud of all that he has become. My love for him is beyond measure.

And to my brothers, Michael and Ken, whose love and encouragement were always the cornerstone of my life. Their love and faith in me have always made me try to be more than I am, more than I thought I could be. I will always be grateful for having the gift of loving them and being loved by them. A sister couldn't ask for more than they have given me or more than they have been to me.

Michael and I lost our brother, Kenny, a couple of years ago, shortly after the first printing of this book came out. His absence has left a huge hole in our hearts; he is loved and missed every day of our lives.

And to my niece, Robyn, who fought the good fight. You were love and light, and you are missed.

SPECIAL ACKNOWLEDGEMENT

A special thank you to Patricia D. Raya who believed in the message of my poems and encouraged me to publish them. She breathed life into this project, nurturing it from the beginning, and going through the labor pains of bringing it into existence. If the title of "mother" could be conferred on someone for going through the birth process of producing a book, it would have to go to her. I couldn't have asked for better support or a harder worker than Patricia.

FORWARD

An Appreciation

Connie H. Deutsch, one who mingles with the Divine. That is what comes to mind when I think about Connie. Knowing this, I feel most fortunate and blessed to help bring to light *Whispers of the Soul*, a collection of meditative poetry written by a woman who exhibits uncommon power for capturing the essence of what it means to be a spiritual being living a human experience.

When I first read *Whispers of the Soul*, I realized it was time for this body of work to be birthed and shared with the many rather than the few. And then September 11th happened, and I knew with deeper conviction that *Whispers of The Soul* had found its time. We are a nation of people in a crisis never seen before in the history of humankind, and we need help. This remarkable body of work gives the reader solace and unbending hope that there are ways to live happily and peacefully through even the most tumultuous times.

Each poetic meditation pierces the veil of illusion that we are separate from the Divine and that hurts cannot heal. Through *Whispers of the Soul*, Connie will gently take you apart and put you back together, piece-by-piece as you explore issues related to abandonment, abuse, sexuality, creativity, greed, jealousy, victimization, and the Divine. Your psychological and spiritual state will never be the same as you submerge and intoxicate yourself in this incredible body of work.

In addition to this beautifully illustrated book, Connie's life's work and spiritual wisdom are now available to the public for the first time in two beautifully narrated audiobooks, workbooks, and a practical home study program. The tools are designed to help the reader realize the truth of who they are and how they can live life with a deeper sense of peace and strength. Join the few who have gone before you and take the evolutionary leap toward liberation, peace, and happiness.

As the world becomes an intricately dependent "global village," I believe that people like Connie and the philosophy represented in *Whispers of the Soul* will not only help transform each of us out of a cultural death spiral, but we will be helped to create a more nurturing culture of individuals who live and love from the Divine seat within. My personal hope for the reader is that *Whispers of the Soul* will beckon you to open the door to your own spiritual journey.

– Patricia D. Raya

TABLE OF CONTENTS

INTRODUCTION

These poems are a chronicle of my spiritual journey. There are times in the life of each of us that we look back over the road we've traveled and reassess where we've been and where we want to go. I'm no exception to that.

It was at a time when I was satisfied with the way things were going for me but I kept feeling that there had to be more. I remembered the song, "Is That All There Is?" and I didn't want to end up like that; I didn't want to reach the end of my life feeling that I had missed the purpose of being here.

I remember the day I made a conscious decision to follow a spiritual path; I didn't discuss it with anyone; I just set about doing it. Now, this doesn't mean that I expected to walk on water or reach the exalted level of ascended Master; it just means that from that point on, I decided to try to be the best person I could be at any given time.

I knew that I would have my good days and my bad days, but I was determined that I would do the best that I could on my bad days and try to do exceedingly well on my good days. It meant that I would continually ask myself if this was the best that I could do or if this was only the best that I had chosen to do. Sometimes, it's the best that I choose to do and I have to make an exerted effort to do the best that I can do, not an easy task for any of us.

I never expected to be saintly; that would have been unrealistic given all my many flaws, but I vowed I would try to be better than I had been. My way of accomplishing this at the time was to take it in very short segments; if something was upsetting, I would allow myself to acknowledge the emotions I was feeling and then I would try to take the higher road.

Sometimes I succeeded and sometimes I did not, but given that I am human, I allowed myself those moments when I was too emotional to rise to the occasion, and afterwards, my thought was that next time I would do better. And again, sometimes I did do better and sometimes I did not, but the key point is that I have never stopped trying.

My concept of a spiritual person is really quite simple; it's predicated on the Golden Rule: Do unto others as you would have others do unto you and also the converse: Do not do to others what you do not want others to do to you. I try to do this in thought, word, and deed, and again, sometimes I succeed and sometimes I do not. It's an uphill battle all the way.

This doesn't mean that I take my spiritual temperature every day. I don't drive myself crazy wondering if the things I am thinking and saying are spiritual; I just live in accordance with the moral code I was taught in my parent's home and try to bring it into every part of my existence. And again, sometimes I succeed and sometimes I do not, but I never stop trying, which is the essence of my commitment to live in accordance with the laws of the universe.

You would think the spiritual path gets easier with time, but in fact, it gets considerably harder because your options are fewer once you become aware of the larger concept.

It means that now when I think an uncharitable thought, I have to stop myself from continuing along that line. If there is a valid grievance, I have to make myself express it verbally, in the best way that I can, doing the least amount of emotional damage that I can.

I try not to stew about a problem but to resolve it through discussion because I know that harboring hostile feelings is against Divine Law, which is the law of love and forgiveness. This is not to be confused with what many New Agers do, which is, that they repress these feelings and pretend that they don't exist.

They speak in terms of "letting it go," when, in fact, they are holding onto it very tightly because of their refusal to acknowledge it and resolve it. There may be times that the other person does not want to hear what you are saying, but it's important that you get the issue out in the open so that it doesn't become a source of sustained anger and resentment.

During the early years of my spiritual journey, I meditated for hours and hours on end, trying to attain God-consciousness as quickly as I could. No one told me that it was an ongoing process that required me to live in my higher self every moment of my life.

I read every book I could get my hands on and evaluated them in terms of where I was in comparison with where the author said I should be. What I discovered was that there were a lot of people writing about the spiritual path, and clearly, they were weren't walking it. They made it seem as though they were perfected beings who were put upon this earth just to point out to the rest of us, the error of our ways.

When reading books like that, you have to be very discerning and separate the message from the messenger. Just like with dieting, you can eat anything you want as long as you don't swallow it all.

This collection of poems was written many years after I started upon the spiritual path. Although they rhyme, I consider them to be more reflective thoughts than poems. They chronicle the feelings of great frustration that I alternately experienced, along with feelings of a very deep connection to God. By turns, I loved Him and was miffed at Him, and praised Him and reproached Him. And the more I tried to understand Him with my finite mind, the more I realized that it's impossible for the finite mind to understand the infinite mind; the rest requires a quantum leap of faith.

Today, I have a deep and abiding love and faith in Him and I question less and believe more because I am continually observing His universal laws in action. Wherever I look, I see Divine Order, and when I try to push too hard to get what I want, and it doesn't happen the way I want it to, I am reminded of that brilliant saying, "Don't push the river; it flows by itself."

At the end of this book, I've included some notes on what I was experiencing at the time I wrote each of these poems and they are reflective of a journey that has taken many years.

The poems in Part One were written almost four decades ago with the exception of a few poems that were written after the September 11th bombings, a decade ago. With the country in turmoil at that time, it seemed only fitting to add Part Two to this book to address the social problems we were facing.

This book would probably never have been written if the poems were not rediscovered by the woman who was editing another book that I was writing. To her, I owe the greatest debt of appreciation for talking me into publishing them because when I reread the words written so many years ago, it felt as though I were setting out upon the path all over again, only this time, a little wiser, a little less naïve, a little more realistic, and a lot more loving and believing. And to God, I owe the greatest thanks of all for being my inspiration and my all-consuming love.

– Connie H. Deutsch

WHISPERS OF THE SOUL

The power of God flows through me
He touches my heart with His love
His band of angels enchant me
With heavenly songs from above.

He comes to me in the stillness
He cleanses my soul with His light
I lift my eyes to His countenance;
I'm struck by the force of His might.

I never thought I'd still be here
I told Him that my time was through
But then He whispered in my ear,
"You still have so much work to do."

So, here I sit and contemplate
And wonder what I've left undone.
He works in such mysterious ways;
I cannot wait till we are One.

THE SEA OF LOVE

My love is like the rolling sea
It flows toward all humanity
It has no form, nor time nor space
It reaches out to every race.

This kind of love does keep one free
It's not constrained by lock and key.
It comforts you with virtue's grace
It is the portrait of God's face.

THE ETERNAL FLAME

I looked within my heart
And waited silently
For You, the Father of my soul
To come and talk to me.

I brushed away the world
Then centered on Your Force
And found the flame that burns within
Unites me with the source.

We had not met in church
Nor temple, mosque, nor shrine,
But in the stillness of my heart
Where You alone, are mine.

We saw the midnight sky
Ablaze with stars and moon,
Illumined by the midday sun
Did disappear too soon.

SONNET TO PAST AND PRESENT LIVES ENTWINED

We've been together in another life
It's strange that we should meet in this one too,
But destiny has moved us three to see
What head, and heart, and will, have come to do.
The three of us are joined by golden cord
Our work was laid out for us from the start,
The strength we need lies in this trinity–
We're bound together by the head and heart.
The energy of this force field is strong
Although our purpose seems at times oblique,
The magnetism that we three produce
Cannot be matched, and makes us quite unique.

The world may someday ask, if it will dare–
What secrets from the past did these three share?

WHEN MOUNTAINS MOVE

When sorrow overwhelms you
And cares have got you down
Don't let your heart despair
Don't let your spirit drown.

I know that you've been through
The dark night of the soul
But now it's time for healing;
It's time to make you whole.

Believe that God will help you
He'll take your cares away.
Amazing things can happen
When you sit down to pray.

Ask and you shall receive
Just lift your voice in song
The tallest mountains move
When faith and hope are strong.

SUNSET MELODY

What a magnificent sight to behold–
Sunset has come with its crimson and gold.
Beauty abounds as the bright shades unfold
Startling the senses with colors so bold.

Galaxies witness this marvelous sight
Wonder and awe are the blends of delight
Look at how nature does play with the light–
Sunset is here; it's the herald of night.

TOUCHED BY GOD

The mountains in their majesty,
The formless clouds go drifting by,
On peaceful days just like today
I know my soul has touched the sky.

The hand of God that leads me on
That doesn't let me fall or fail
That picks me up when I am down
Has led me to the Holy Grail.

He fills my soul; I do not yearn
His presence makes me feel complete
No matter where I go in life
I see God's face in all I meet.

I cannot judge; I can't condemn
For then I could not keep God near
Were I to throw just one small stone
The God within would disappear.

So when I meet you in the street
I'll see a soul that's pure and good.
I'll know that you've been touched by God
His words of love, now understood.

THE TEACHER

The teacher only opens doors;
She shows the way, the truth, the light.
And then the student finds the switch
That makes his inner soul burn bright.

The teacher plants her seeds of truth
Upon her student's fertile mind,
Then silently withdraws from view
To watch his goals become defined.

The student goes from dark to light
Within a year or two, and then
Becomes engulfed in doubts and fears
And struggles to begin again.

It's not an easy path to choose,
For you must walk this road alone.
Your teacher sets you on your way
With faith and hope as stepping-stones.

But inner conflicts rise and fall;
Her words grow dim and fade away.
Then suddenly, the God within
Reveals Himself to you one day.

DREAMS

I dreamt that you were here again;
You had not gone away.
We had the years ahead of us;
Now gone in just a day.

We planned a lot, the two of us;
There was no way to know,
That God would call you back to
Him 'Ere I could let you go.

I look for reasons but I fail
To see the sense in this
That you were taken from my life,
Rewarded with God's kiss.

But if you had to go, my dear,
If we must be apart,
It comforts me that you're with God;
You both have claimed my heart.

I know I must get on with life,
So here I sit and pray,
For inner strength and fortitude
To get me through the day.

I'm lucky that my faith is strong;
I'll soon come out to play.
For now I'm just content to wait
Until God shows the way.

MIRACLES

Miracles are what I see
Looking at the sky and sea.
How exciting this can be
Giving proof of God to me.

Waterfalls and rivers, too,
Sparkling shades of green and blue
All creation gives a clue,
Seeing God in all we do.

Miracles are everywhere
Nature calls me out to hear
Songs of life sung true and clear
When God whispers in my ear.

When my soul is flying free
Past the robins in the trees
Miracles are what I see–
Knowing God is touching me.

SUSPENDED IN TIMELESSNESS

We dance around the edges of reality
Playing with fragmented bits of truths.
We sing and chant and talk of immortality
Hoping that its music really soothes.

How can we know the soul moves through eternity
If we measure time in passing years?
How can we see God's special creativity
If our inner faith gives way to fears?

The spirit that connects us dwells in purity
Heritage assures us of our love.
When we are linked to God's remarkability
We're transported on the wings of doves.

LOVE'S GREATEST JOY

A mother has no greater joy on Earth
Than seeing how her child's grown through the years;
For then she knows the measure of her worth–
The love reflected in his smiles and tears.
His tiny hands once felt upon her face,
And she, caressing him with just a look
Recalls his voice was like a warm embrace–
His sparkling laughter, like a bubbling brook.
Now boyhood's gone and he's become a man,
Discovering that life's not what it seems.
From deep within his soul there comes a plan–
With dauntless courage he pursues his dreams.

His destiny is where his heart abides–
A mother's love is where her child resides.

MIDNIGHT MEMORIES

Moments of memory vanish in time
Scrapbook of treasures forgotten with age
Gone are the happenings dimmed by the years
Picturesque pieces torn out of the page.

What do we see with such crystal-clear sight?
Is it still with us the moment it's past?
Why does it linger through a glass darkly?
How do we hold it to make it all last?

Yesterday's scene is now far out of view
Nothing worth keeping can be held too tight
Gone are the memories we once held so dear
Everything vanishes into the night.

MIDNIGHT MELODIES

In the stillness of the night
When the Earth has closed its eyes,
I sit down to visualize
How the rhapsodies take flight.
As I write by candlelight
All the rhythms that I hear–
Midnight melodies appear.

Strains of music come to mind
As I watch the starlight's glare
Shattered silence cuts the air.
Strike the chord for humankind
If you listen, you will find
Orchestrations everywhere–
Midnight melodies appear.

TREE OF FRIENDSHIP

My friends are like the great oak tree
Their character is firm and tall
Whose branches reach out, sheltering me
With love and caring, giving all.

We plant the seeds of tree and friend
And watch them flourish with the years
With gentle strength, a perfect blend
The face of love that friendship wears.

There are no debts; we keep no score
We understand each other's needs
We help each other strive for more
Our hearts entwined with loving deeds.

THE HAND OF GOD

The essence of life
Is like a ship's helm;
It's all in God's hands–
Divinity's realm.

Our home is the Earth–
Above are the stars.
Creation abounds–
Divinity's ours.

God gave us free will
To choose what is right,
And then blessed us with–
Divinity's light.

DIADEM OF HOPE

When I'm about my Father's work in prayer
And meditation for the day is done
The ocean of my cares is swept aside–
The sea of consciousness and I are one.

What I would give to see His countenance–
To have Him show me what I should be seeing,
To meet the loving Father of my soul
In whom I live and move and have my being.

He crowns me with a diadem of hope
Then gives me second sight to see within.
He warns me to be gentle with their souls
And bids me speak of love and not of sin.

"What is the nature of the soul?" I ask,
"When will we be a part of Your great plan?"
It's then I hear His voice within me saying,
"When you're more loving to your fellow man."

THE COSMIC PATH

The path is narrow that I walk
With options few and far between
But oh, what joy does fill my soul
When God and I sit down to talk.

My heart is bursting at the seams
To feel the love I have for God
It carries me to distant heights
And far surpasses all my dreams.

It's at those times I take no part
In things I know bring karmic woes;
Forgiveness is the Law of Grace
Encompassed by a loving heart.

A FRIEND IS FOREVER

Good friends are like rare wines–
The older they get, the dearer their value.
They can be served to royalty because they are, in truth,
The kings and queens of humanity.

They stand out in memory because time is their ally,
Mellowing them more exquisitely with each passing year.
A small drop of a rare vintage friend–
Enough to inebriate the soul.

You, dear friend, are that noble wine.
Let me inhale your beautiful bouquet,
Imbibe the taste of your fruit and
Sip from the goblet of your everlasting friendship.

WITHIN ME

The flame burns bright within my soul
The still small voice within me speaks.
There is no need to go outside –
The God within has made me whole.

If there were no such thing as sin
And paradise were here on earth –
Contentment would be ecstasy –
Transcended bliss of God within.

What would this life appear to be
If I had all except my soul?
How gladly I would give it up
To have the God within, keep me.

TWILIGHT FLIGHT

In the twilight of my years
How my soul has longed to be
Like a bluebird soaring high
Ever upward, freeing me.
I would like before I die
To be rid of earthly fears.

Life is mixed with joy and tears
All you have is what you see
Most events go rushing by
Still, I'm yearning to be free.
How I wish my soul could fly
In the twilight of my years.

THE MASK OF LIFE

The heart of one has gently wooed
The mystery of life's pursuit.
The fertile mind bears golden fruit;
The soul shines forth at once renewed.

There is no time nor space for me
There can be no such thing as death.
There only is the life and breath;
There will we find infinity.

When all our questions have been asked
When can we hope and plan and scheme?
When will we find all of our dreams?
When all of life has been unmasked.

THE RAINBOW BRIDGE

I've walked along the rainbow bridge
Footloose and fancy-free
Absorbing seven colored rays–
Uniting God with me.

I've journeyed far along this path
Through all eternity;
While meditating on God's form,
I've glimpsed infinity.

I've traveled up and down this road
To try to get to be
A paragon in human form
Of love and harmony.

I've blazed a trail to heaven's gate
To seek the golden key,
Unlocking secrets of my soul–
Uniting God with me.

TO BETTER DAYS

If memories are all that you have left
Of how life casts its shadow on your floor,
Then see your image in a heart bereft
Of hidden joys that stole out through your door.
Self-pity pinned you to the netherworld
And bitterly, you bathed your face in tears.
You waved your flag of martyrdom, unfurled
For all the world to mourn your wasted years.
And day by day, you let life pass you by
Afraid to die, but more afraid to live
For if you live, then you must satisfy
The soul within, by learning to forgive.

So, come, my dear, before it's all destroyed;
The days grow short, and life's to be enjoyed.

MOONBEAM MAGIC

When moonbeams play upon the lawn,
I see the elves and pixies laugh.
They work and sing the whole night long
And then they disappear at dawn.

The moonbeams cast their magic spell
When all the world is fast asleep.
They bounce around with carefree ease
Like fairies in the grassy dell.

Enchanted forests dressed in green–
The Elementals holding court–
And somewhere in the still of night
Are moonbeams dancing in between.

When daybreak comes, they all adjourn–
The playful pixies now are gone
The moonbeams vanish with the light–
Tomorrow night they will return.

TO THE PLANET NEPTUNE

Elusive Neptune casts its spell
In oh, so many ways.
You fool yourself; you think you're well–
The games that Neptune plays.

The fog rolls in; you cannot see–
It weaves its tangled web.
The ecstasy, the misery,
Emotions flow and ebb.

Delusive Neptune skulks about
With anesthetic care,
Illusion cloaked in dreamy doubt
It cautions you– Beware!

CELESTIAL FANTASY

I dreamt I walked among the stars
To Venus, Jupiter, and Mars.
Galactic travel was for me
In this celestial fantasy.

I looked around and plainly spied
A way that I could get to ride
With fairy queens and elfin kings
For on my back were angel's wings.

We stopped among the elves and sprites
And watched them beam their colored lights.
The Elementals did agree
That we had shared a fantasy.

I knew that Earth would claim me soon
I'd have to leave the stars and moon
But now I wanted it to be
One more celestial fantasy.

DO I HAVE A CHOICE?

If all we see, we've seen it not,
If all we hear, we've soon forgot
Then all we have in this short life
Is empty toil and useless strife.

TOMORROW'S DREAM

We stalk the shadows of the night
In dreamlike reverie,
We walk between the dark and light
Not knowing what we see.

The world lays out its banquet spread
For all of us to eat
But still there are the underfed
Of those afraid to eat.

Life offers us its wide array
Of everything we need,
And yet we live in yesterday
Because of selfish greed.

How can we plant tomorrow's dream
Without the seed of chance?
When we risk naught, it always seems
The piper plays – we dance.

MOONLIGHT BECOMES YOU

Moonlight becomes you–
It shines on your hair,
It lights up your face,
It shows you in prayer,
A portrait of grace;
In all that you do–
Moonlight becomes you.

OUT IN SPACE

On the plane to parts unknown
Gazing out beyond the clouds
Wondering what it's like out there
Far above the bustling crowds.

Should I leave this soaring jet?
Should I leave my body, too,
Unrestrained and free to roam
With the sun and skies of blue?

On the plane to parts unknown
Nighttime has approached too soon.
Here I sit and contemplate,
Walking with the stars and moon.

MY HEART REMEMBERS

My heart remembers when we met
Of how we loved and laughed and shared
You were the one who mattered most,
You were the one who really cared.

Now you are gone; I cannot dwell
On what I'll never know again.
You're in my thoughts, my mind, my soul,
You're in my heart since time began.

We'll meet again; of that I'm sure
You are my love, my destiny.
My heart remembers that you were
Kissed by God, and kissed by me.

I won't forget the joy you gave
Or how God filled our life anew.
I must give thanks for what we had
And how my heart remembers you.

APPENDIX

Whispers of the Soul

I'm the introspective type and, several years ago, I turned inward to examine my life for the umpteenth time. I looked at the goals I had once set for myself and realized that I had reached them all and that there was nothing else that I wanted to achieve.

This set me to thinking that my life was probably coming to an end. Being the organized person that I am, I immediately began to put my personal and professional affairs in order and then I went about my work thinking that the end was near.

When several months passed and nothing had happened, I was kind of miffed with God. It was like the expression, "All dressed up and nowhere to go." I either wanted to do something significant or I didn't see the point of hanging around. The fact that I'm still here, makes me question what I've left undone.

The Sea of Love

It is one thing to vilify a person for what he has done, but it's another thing to persecute someone for his beliefs, skin color, religion, or nationality.

I have watched people go to their house of worship and pray to their God for forgiveness, and before the day was through, mistreat someone because he belonged to a different religion or had a different skin color. It was as if these people were proclaiming to the world, if you do things my way, then you're spiritual; if you believe something different or if you look different, then you're not spiritual.

This isn't spirituality, it's prejudice; it's narrow-minded people who are too intolerant of others to live and let live. When I wrote this poem, I was trying to imagine what the face of God looked like and I decided that it is unconditional love that defines His face.

The Eternal Flame

One day in meditation, I experienced the sensation of being bathed in a circle of light. As I sat there with my eyes closed, I had a vision of a midnight sky, the moon, and billions of brightly lit stars, and right there, in the center of this, was the brightness of the midday sun shining so brightly over the night sky that everything stood out in stark relief.

It was the most magnificent thing I had ever seen and my first thought was that if everyone could see this, there would never be wars or hatred; there would only be infinite love.

Sonnet to Past and Present Lives Entwined

People come into our life for a day, a week, a year, or a lifetime, and we don't usually know the reason while it's happening. Sometimes, it's to help us through a difficult time or to teach us a lesson; sometimes it's in response to our prayers; sometimes it's for us to share what we have, to grow, or to be the instrument of someone else's lesson. For whatever reason, the people who march in and out of our lives enrich our lives in some way.

A few decades ago, two men entered my life for a very brief time. We went everywhere together; we were mentally challenged, shared the same sense of humor, and enjoyed each other's company, and then they were gone.

I am a very strong reincarnationist and believe in karma and past lives; I don't think these two men shared those beliefs. I felt a very strong karmic link with them but in a most unusual way. When I was with one of them, the link was muted, but when the three of us were together, it was as if there was a force greater than the three of us, magnetically pulling us together toward something indefinable. I didn't question what I was feeling but I did record it in this poem.

When Mountains Move

After the September 11th bombings, so many people who had already been diagnosed as clinically depressed, became even more depressed than usual. They had a very difficult time functioning, and their fears took on an even greater magnitude. Businesses were losing money, the nation was afraid of terrorism coming to our shores, and people were losing their life savings and retirement funds in the stock market.

It has not been a stable environment for our countrymen and this poem reflects the need for us to heal individually, and as a nation. When things are at their worst, the need to hope and have faith that a force greater than ourselves is at work, is essential to moving on with our lives.

When we believe in nothing, we will have nothing. When we believe that something will happen and desire it with an intense passion, we can make it manifest and become our reality.

Sunset Melody

One autumn, when I was out of town, I was so captivated by the changing leaves that I wrote this poem. They were so magnificent that I stood there spellbound. The red and orange leaves, with the sun shining brightly through them, looked as though they were setting the sky on fire.

In those moments before sundown, everything looked vibrant and alive; the purples were deeper, the yellows, oranges, and reds were brighter, and the landscape came alive with the profusion of colors.

Touched by God

During the holidays, I was with my family and feeling peaceful. I felt this deep connection to God and all was right with my world. Over the years, no matter how bad things have been, I've always managed to get through the worst of times.

The years have taught me that God will always help me if I turn to Him, and if I live in accordance with Divine law, my life will run smoothly.

One of these laws is to not speak badly of others, and I have found that when I disobey that law, I am not able to feel that deep connection to God. Since this is my prime motivator in life, I make an effort to visualize the God within each person as often as I can because I know that each of us is made in the image of God, and that this God-self is within each of us.

The Teacher

When I first started out on my spiritual path, I wanted to attain God-consciousness NOW. I went to meditation classes and asked my teacher a million questions. Although she was very patient with me, she didn't have the answers I was seeking.

I was far less patient; I wanted to know everything and I wanted to know how to apply the knowledge, and, of course, I wanted it instantly. I read everything I could get my hands on and went to every lecture that sounded interesting.

Still, wherever I went for answers, no one had enough to satisfy me; they didn't even have enough for themselves.

At the time, I thought my teacher could imbue me with this mystical spirituality and I was keenly disappointed to discover she didn't have that power.

The first year was truly exciting. Every time I

meditated, I would be treated to a visual smorgasbord. I'd see my past lives; I'd also see the faces of some of the ascended Masters or have precognitive visions. In my naïveté, I thought this would last forever and ever. I couldn't have been more wrong.

All of a sudden, the visions stopped. I no longer saw faces of the ascended Masters, or places like the Taj Mahal. I stopped having precognitive visions and I no longer saw my past lives. In short, I felt like I was living in a spiritual wasteland. It was dreadful. I wanted that symbolic reassurance that I was becoming more spiritual with every foray into meditation, and none was forthcoming.

The next decade was a frustrating time of my life and this poem depicts the struggle I was having. I didn't want to be my own teacher; I wanted to have a teacher guide me, to hand me a road map of my spiritual journey that I could follow like a paint by number picture.

And I was miffed with God for taking away my road signs and making me find Him without any help. Eventually, it became patently obvious to me that no one can confer spirituality on you; you have to do that for yourself.

I had to learn that a teacher can only open doors; she can show the way, the truth, and the light, but the student has to do the rest. I also had to learn to go within for my own answers and not depend on anyone else to supply them because no one knows my needs better than I.

Dreams

The September 11th bombings left all of us a little shell-shocked. We clung together as a nation and mourned the loss of the men and women who lost their lives that morning; we also mourned the loss of our innocence, the shattered feelings of security that we used to have when we thought we lived in the most powerful country in the world.

Now we know that no one's safety is guaranteed and no country is beyond the reach of terrorism. Most of us have suffered loss in some way, at some time in our lives, and have had to find a way to carry on, but very few of us have had to do it with the rest of the world watching us.

These reflective thoughts were written for everyone who has ever lost a loved one, but most especially for those who lost their loved ones on that memorable day.

Miracles

I wrote this poem in response to the many people who were questioning the existence of God. I kept hearing things like "If there really is a God, He wouldn't let bad things happen to good people. . . If there really is a God, He wouldn't allow wars, poverty, sickness, etc. . . I would believe that there is a God if I had some proof, if He performed some miracles like He did in the days of biblical times."

My absolute belief in God has nothing to do with personal miracles. For me, every time I look up and see the changing shapes of the clouds as they move slowly across the sky, I am witness to another of God's miracles.

Where do the mountains come from? or the rivers and streams? Where do our emotions come from? Where does love come from? Everywhere I look, I see God's miracles in evidence and they all touch the deepest part of my soul.

Suspended in Timelessness

This poem represents a dark, murky time in my life when my meditations were so devoid of the visions I had once experienced, that I was sure I couldn't possibly be feeling a connection to God.

For two years, while I wrestled with the absence of incontrovertible proof that I was truly on a spiritual path, I kept running into "phony holies."

These people were either running all over the world chasing after gurus who could grant them instant God-consciousnes just from being in their presence, or they were pseudo-gurus, who talked endlessly about spirituality but didn't live it. I watched them talk the talk without walking the talk; their message was clear: "do as I say, not as I do."

At some point, I realized that this was all about faith; you can't be proclaiming your faith in God if you are worrying about not being able to pay your bills. I reasoned that if I was doing everything possible to earn a living, and

I was still coming up short, I had to leave it up to God to find a way for me to cover the shortfall.

I decided to test my theory that my problems represented a rubber band; if I give one end of the rubber band to God and He starts pulling on it, and I take the other end of the rubber band and pull on it, too, I would be fighting God and He would withdraw His help because it would look like I didn't need it. I figured if I'm supposed to be on a spiritual path, then I'd better learn how to have absolute faith in God.

One day, when my bills were staring me in the face and I was scared because I didn't know where the next dollar was coming from, I said, "OK, God, I'm leaving this in Your hands. These are the bills I need to pay and this is the latest date I can pay them. And then I made myself stop worrying.

Whenever my mind would drift toward those unpaid bills, I would force myself to say, "God will take care of it" and then I would think about something else. The day before those bills were due, I received a check from an insurance company for an accident I had had many years before and had completely forgotten about. The check covered all my bills and there was twenty-five cents left over.

Love's Greatest Joy

This poem was written for my son, who has always been my greatest joy. Of all the things I have accomplished in this life, the most noteworthy and most gratifying of all, has been giving birth to him and having him in my life.

He has grown into a man who holds himself to the highest degree of integrity, while also embodying a wealth of love, compassion, and wisdom. He is loved and admired by his family and friends, and most especially, by me.

Midnight Memories

Memories can be so elusive. We think we remember a person or event with such crystal-clear accuracy, but we really don't. As time passes, our memories become distorted.

Eye-witnesses at the scene of an accident will give their version of what happened, and a year later, when they are called to testify in court, their answers don't match their original statements. So, too, when we try to hold onto the depth of an emotion, the intensity can't be sustained, either.

Extreme moments of sadness and exuberance will only last a few minutes and, like our memories, the more we try to hold onto them, the more they will recede.

Midnight Melodies

There has always been a sense of mystery about the night. It feels like the most spiritual time because all the hustle and bustle of the day is gone; the world is asleep and you're awake, and no one can intrude upon your thoughts.

This is the most creative time. One often hears music that does not appear in his everyday life; it only comes in the wee hours of the morning. If there is ever a perfect time to meditate on God, it's in the stillness of the night.

Tree of Friendship

My friends have been the one constant, and the biggest blessing in my life. Together with my family, they are the ones I can count on to be with me through the good times and the bad times.

Throughout the years, we have supported each other emotionally, celebrating each other's successes, and commiserating with each other in times of hardship; we are fortunate to have reaped the seeds of love that were planted so many years ago.

The Hand of God

There have been many disagreements about free will, karma, and the essence of life. It is often said that the theory of karma and reincarnation obviates our free will. I believe in both, free will and the law of karma, and that they are not mutually exclusive.

I think of us as having free will, but karmically, that free will is on a short leash. In other words, our higher self knows what is right, and with the free will that God has granted us, we can choose to live in accordance with Divine law or we can choose to separate ourselves from God.

No matter what choices we make, the law of karma is in operation and we can reap either positive karma or negative karma based on our actions.

Diadem of Hope

This poem describes a very busy time in my life when I was trying to find my way in the world while embarking on a spiritual journey. My only freedom and inner peace came about through meditation, and therefore, I spent all my spare time meditating on God and trying to raise my consciousness. I yearned for that awakening and tried to understand the nature of the soul.

During one of those meditations, I heard an inner voice telling me that people are more concerned about committing sins than about their capacity to love, and that the connection between the soul and God is the ability to love one's fellow man without standing in judgment.

I had often asked God to allow me to see into the hearts and minds of people so I could help them heal their souls and find happiness. In another meditation, I was shown that the way to acquire this second sight was for me to go beyond the concept of sin and connect with the Divine spark that is within each of us.

The Cosmic Path

A vision quest is a solitary undertaking. It's not the kind of thing you discuss with others, at least not at a very deep level, so your communication is mostly with God.

Some people think of a vision quest as going off by yourself to sit on top of a mountain or set up camp in a forest for several days until you receive a vision. For me, it's been an ongoing process that has spanned four decades.

Awareness comes slowly; it's not a blinding epiphany. Little by little, you realize that it's not good enough to talk about the Law of Grace; you have to be proactive in bringing it into your life. It's relatively easy to not lie and cheat, but it's more of a challenge to not gossip, not condemn others for their human foibles, and to be loving and forgiving to all who walk the earth.

When you are not very evolved, you can get away with a lot. If you are very evolved and have chosen the path of spirituality, your options are much more limited.

An unevolved person is analogous to someone who is wearing a brown robe; when mud spatters all over it, it's barely noticeable. A very evolved person is akin to someone who is wearing a white robe; when even the smallest mud spot lands on it, everyone can see it. So, too, when an unevolved person gossips and decimates reputations, it's not critical to his evolvement, but when a very evolved person gossips and ruins someone's reputation, he loses that connection to God.

When a person makes a conscious decision to pursue a spiritual path, he soon discovers that it is a very narrow path and that he is walking it alone; he is doing it for himself, not for public acclaim.

A Friend is Forever

One day I was taking stock of the many blessings in my life and I realized, for the zillionth time, that I have been very lucky in my friendships. Most of them have lasted several decades and we have weathered the storms of life together, providing each other with love and an emotional safe haven.

I include my family in this grouping; they have been the best of friends, the kings and queens of humanity who have enriched my life beyond my wildest dreams and have been my staunchest supporters.

Within Me

This poem represents a time in my life when my principles were being sorely tested. I often had to choose between my next meal and standing up for my principles; my principles always won.

To this day, I would gladly give up all my material goods if it ever came to a choice between feeling that deep connection to God, and having everything else of a material value.

Twilight Flight

Fear is a crippling emotion and is the greatest deterrent to personal freedom. There are so many aspects to it: fear of rejection, fear of success, fear of failure, fear of anything, that it paralyzes a person into inertia and explains why so many people are rigid and resistant to change.

I find it interesting that the ones who are so proud of their stubbornness and who wear it like a badge of honor don't realize that fear is the underlying cause of their refusal to change. It is also one of the prime causes of procrastination although one would never consciously make that kind of connection.

Fear is the greatest stumbling block to someone expressing anger and explains why so many people avoid confrontations. Sometimes the fear is so overpowering that a person cannot express even a scintilla of the anger he feels because the words are locked inside and can't come out.

When the fury is that intense, the person will either become explosive and start shouting, cursing, or throwing things, or he will freeze up and let the anger implode, so that it turns inward and stays there within his body where it eventually becomes a disease.

Whenever I run across someone who is a chameleon or a people-pleaser, I immediately know that this is a person who is afraid to take emotional risks as well as being afraid to let people see his real self; he is afraid of saying or doing anything that might offend someone. For this type of person, it's peace at any price.

No matter what it costs in self-esteem or dignity, he does everything he can to avoid difficult confrontations, even going so far as to deceive himself by downplaying the situation so that he doesn't have to act on it. This person desperately wants to be liked; he wants to please everyone, and above all, he is protecting himself from the possibility of being rejected.

Many people are afraid to face their inner self so they make themselves too busy to stop long enough to get to the root of their unhappiness. These are the people who never have an extra minute.

They make sure they're "over-scheduled" and "under-timed" with either work or social commitments, or both.

One of the most crippling fears is the one that revolves around financial security. I have seen people miserable in their jobs, hating their bosses and/or coworkers, suffering the backlash of discrimination, or being passed over for promotions and pay raises, and yet the fear of being without a job or having to interview for another job, even if it is a much better job involving more pay and a better benefits package, can be so traumatic to the employee that he is too paralyzed to look for a job that gives him greater opportunities.

The Mask of Life

Many people believe strongly in reincarnation and karma and they speak about death as being a wonderful entry into immortality, as though by the physical death, they are merely walking through another door of life.

They speak about crying when someone is born because they know that the person came here to fulfill his karma and that he will likely have much sadness in his life; they speak of celebrating when someone dies because it means that his soul has accomplished what it set out to do and he is free to leave the earth for this incarnation.

Someone once said that Christians believe in the immortality of the soul, that the soul never dies and that when the body dies, the soul enters the kingdom of heaven; yet no one seems to be in a great hurry to get there. There has been so much talk about the immortal soul by believers and non-believers alike; many people ask questions of God but few people sit still long enough to hear His answers. God knows the real person inside of us, our strengths and our weaknesses. There is no need for the masks that people wear; there is no need to have an inner and outer persona, the public and the private person.

Before someone can be united with God, he has to be real enough to take off his masks and stand before his maker as God created him, in purity and love.

The Rainbow Bridge

Meditation has been called the Rainbow Bridge because it is a bridging in consciousness between the lower mind and the higher mind and it corresponds to the seven colored rays associated with the seven planes of consciousness.

This bridging relates the individual mind to the higher mind, and eventually, to the Universal Mind; it is the bridging between the personality and the soul.

Man has to make a conscious effort to bridge the gap between personality and spirit, to reach the plane of God-consciousness.

To Better Days

I've met some people who play the martyr to the hilt. No one could feel as sorry for them as they feel for themselves. They spend so much of their lives wallowing in self-pity, that they never allow themselves to feel real happiness, even when it's there for the taking.

There's an old expression that describes these people: "he's only happy when he's miserable." And then there are those who are afraid to live. They're so afraid to take risks and reach for the proverbial brass ring, it's almost as if they are already dead. How then, can we acknowledge their actual death, if we have never seen evidence that they lived?

Life is short; we shouldn't waste a moment of it because no one knows how much time we have left. We need to live life to the fullest and live every day as though it were our last. Jonathan Swift summed it up very well when he wrote, "May you live all the days of your life."

Moonbeam Magic

I once heard about a woman who had taken a picture of a grassy knoll and when she had her Kodak film developed, there were very clear pictures of fairies playing in the area. Since then, I've read of a few instances where people have seen them and captured them on film.

Alas, I have not seen any fairies, nor do I have pictures of them on film, but my imagination sees them, even if my film does not.

To the Planet, Neptune

I once attended an Astrology lecture on the planet, Neptune. The lecturer had said that Neptune is the planet of illusion, and wherever it is placed in a chart, that's where the person has a difficult time seeing reality.

During a Neptune transit, a person's sense of reality is often distorted, and mistaken illusions, confusion, doubt, and fear can arise. The flip side of this transit is that you can feel exhilarated and at one with the entire universe and you can dedicate your life to making the world a better place.

It's also advised that you don't make permanent commitments during this transit as you may not have all the pertinent facts at your disposal.

Celestial Fantasy

I once read an illustrated book about angels. In it, were pictures of tree and mountain Devas (the nature spirits); the earth Elementals (beings whose bodies are composed of the elements in which they live); the Solar

Logos (the sun, the most advanced Initiate of our solar system); and the different types of angels.

William Blake, the poet, is said to have seen angels standing in a tree by a roadside when he was a boy, and as an adult, he saw Presences in the earth and air who were interested in man's destiny.

The angel book spoke about these Divine spirits at work and at play and my imagination took flight and I had to write about them. Mt. Olympus, with its legendary powers written about in mythology, is the tallest mountain peak in Greece and was named by the Turkish people, the "Abode of the Celestials." It was too good a title to waste, so I borrowed the "Celestials" part for the title of my poem, "Celestial Fantasy."

Do I Have a Choice?

There are many people who go through life oblivious to everything that doesn't pertain to them. They take their relationships and their possessions for granted, neither noticing nor appreciating what they have. The only problems that affect them are their own; they barely notice the trials and tribulations of anyone else.

These self-absorbed people forget that there is a connection between them and others, because their main concern is themselves. What they don't understand is that the less connected they are to mankind, the less connected they are to God.

Tomorrow's Dream

We always hear people talking about wanting to make vast changes in their life, yet so few people are willing to take those first steps.

There are usually more options available to us than we realize but if our attitude is that we're better off with the devil we know, than the angel we fear, we'll never have the courage to explore those opportunities.

We've all seen people who have been shown something better, and even shown how they can accomplish the transition, yet there is so much fear of the unknown that they stay rooted in their unhappiness.

When a person is too paralyzed by fear to take risks, very little comes to him; he is always at the mercy of others and has to dance to their tune.

Moonlight Becomes You

There's something special about the way a person looks silhouetted in the moonlight, with the light limning the figure against the darkness. There's an otherworldly appearance to it that feels mystical, and the quiet of the night lends a magical enchantment.

Out in Space

The plane trip was long. As I sat there, looking out of the window, we lifted into the air and flew over the city, making the houses below us look like the wooden pieces on a Monopoly board.

We soared above the clouds in a bright, sunshiny, sky, and there was such an exhilarating feeling of freedom that I wondered what it would be like to experience flying without the physical limitations of a body that had to sit in a plane.

Then the sky slowly darkened and we flew towards sunset, and then into nighttime, and this time, when I thought about flying solo, I thought about being so high up in the sky that I could almost reach out and touch the stars and moon.

My Heart Remembers

I wasn't even thinking about writing a poem but the words just kept playing in my head until I had to do something with them. I think it started shortly after the September 11th bombings.

I kept wanting to DO something to help the families of the men and women who had lost their lives, but there was nothing I could do, so I just continued doing my counseling and helping people deal with their depression on a personal level, and helping them deal with the awful consequences of terrorism on their businesses.

From time to time, I would think about the lives lost and how those people will be remembered by their loved ones, and the title of the poem, "My Heart Remembers," came into my mind. Then, a few nights later, as I was driving around in the middle of the night, the words of the first stanza of the poem took shape in my mind. I pulled off to the side of the road to write them down and hurried home to finish the poem.

ABOUT THE AUTHOR

Connie H. Deutsch is an author, renowned consultant and spiritual advisor who has a keen understanding of human nature and is a natural problem-solver. She is known throughout the world for helping clients find workable solutions to problems that are often complex and systemic in nature and part of a corporation's culture or an individual's pattern of behavior.

Connie's depth of experience lends itself to both corporate consulting and individual counseling. Perhaps Connie is best known for her "homework" assignments which serve as virtual road maps for moving clients through problems into living solutions.

In addition to her consulting and counseling practice, Connie has hosted her own weekly radio show, is a regular contributor to the spiritual and personal growth website *Next Level Soul* (www.nextlevelsoul.com) and is one of the most downloaded guests ever on the popular *Next Level Soul with Alex Ferrari* podcast.

She has been a guest on numerous cable, radio shows, and podcasts around the country. She wrote a weekly advice column for sixteen years and has been has been invited to speak at universities around the world.

Visit her website at www.ConnieHDeutsch.com

next level SOUL™

Next Level Soul™ is a resource for spiritual seekers, and curious souls who are looking to find the deeper meaning in their lives. On NLS you will learn from some of the world's top spiritual and thought leaders. To help you on your spiritual path NLS publishes books, audiobooks, courses, weekly podcasts, and videos. We are here to help you on your life's journey and awaken your inner peace.

Next Level Soul™ founder, Alex Ferrari is a #1 best-selling author, speaker, entrepreneur, award-winning filmmaker, spiritual seeker and podcaster. His industry leading podcasts, the Webby award-nominated Indie Film Hustle, and Bulletproof Screenwriting have been downloaded over 11 million times to date. He has had the pleasure of speaking to icons like Oscar® Winner *Oliver Stone* and *Billy Crystal,* music legends like *Bruce Dickinson* (Iron Maiden) and *Moby* (Grammy® Award Winning Music Icon), actors like *Edward Burns* (Saving Private Ryan) and *Eva Longoria* (Desperate Housewives), thought leaders like 2X Noble Prize Nominee *Dr. Ervin Laszlo* and *Dr. Eben Alexander* (Proof of Heaven) and New York Times Best-Selling authors Dan Millman (The Way of the Peaceful Warrior) and Dr. Raymond Moody (Life After Life).

Throughout his life's journey Alex was always asking the big questions. Why are we here? Is this all there is? What is my soul's mission in this life? He developed NLS to help people around the world get closer to their own higher power; to look inward for the answers they are searching for.

The *Next Level Soul™ Podcast* was created to help answer those questions by having raw and inspiring conversations with some of the most fascinating and thought provoking souls on the planet today.

For more information on Next Level Soul:

Official Site: www.nextlevelsoul.com

Next Level Soul Podcast: www.nextlevelsoul.com/podcast

Next Level Soul Books: www.nextlevelsoul.com/books

THOUGHTS AND REFLECTIONS

I wanted to create a space for you to write down your thoughts and reflections after reading sections of the book. Think of this as your own personal addition to the book. Look inside yourself and write down what you are feeling right now. You will thank yourself in the future.

_____

_____

_____

_____

_____

_____

_____

_____

_____

_____

_____

_____

_____

_____

_____

_____

_____

_____

_____

_____

_____

_____

_____

_____

_____

_____

_____